Y0-BZZ-645

Ylla

Animals

in India

Text and photographs by Ylla

Layout and design by Luc Bouchage

Harper & Brothers Publishers

New York

Printed in Switzerland, by Héliographia S. A., Lausanne

Ylla went to India to photograph the animal life of that vast country as she had done previously in Africa. Material for Animals in India *was gathered over a period of seven months in many parts of India. Ylla was winding up her trip photographing a country fair in Bharatpur when an accident took her life.*

In addition to her photographs Ylla left three notebooks in which she had made almost daily entries from the time she landed in New Delhi until the day before her death. The notes were not kept for the purpose of publication. They were maintained as a private record of her impressions and described the circumstances under which her pictures were taken.

From this diary the following notes were selected and edited as a valuable and colorful testimony to her own experience.

En route to India, August 1954

It was Jean Renoir, director of the film *The River*, who actually prompted me to go to India. This was last summer, when I was staying with my friends, the Pierre Sicards, in Bel Air, California, and we saw Renoir very often.

It had, in fact, been my childhood dream to be invited by a maharaja, and to see a white elephant, but I never dreamed it would be enough to send a book of mine to an eastern prince, and in return, receive an invitation. That is precisely what happened. I mailed my *Animals in Africa* to the Maharaja of Mysore, a great enthusiast of both wildlife and photography, and shortly after, I had a telephone call from Mac,[1] who told me that a registered letter had arrived for me from His Highness of Mysore, in care of Harper's. The letter contained an invitation.

Months of preparation followed: customs, letters of introduction, research, much reading, and contacting people who had been there. From them, as well as from Barbara Flaherty Van Ingen[2] with whom I had carried on a correspondence, I received generally discouraging reports about wildlife in India.

New Delhi, August 1954

At the Crafts and Industry Show, I met Mr. Nehru's daughter, Mrs. Indira Gandhi. She told me of her three pandas, at present in the hills to escape the heat—pandas cannot bear a hot climate. I sent Mrs. Gandhi copies of my book on Africa, and *The Sleepy Little Lion*. The following day I received a charming note from her in which she thanked me for the books (it seems she has had a copy of *The Sleepy Little Lion* in a

[1] Frank MacGregor, Chairman of the Board of Harper & Brothers.

[2] Daughter of Robert Flaherty, Barbara has lived in Mysore for some years.

French version since 1948), and invited me to look at slides of the pandas. They turned out to be enchanting. I was actually tempted to take the train to the hills (Nandital) where the pandas are during the summer months. But it is a long trip—a night and half a day—and it might easily rain there. I decided to try my luck with the pandas when I return to Delhi from the South.

Indira Gandhi is exceedingly fond of animals. She had a deer, she told me, when she was a little girl. The deer had the unfortunate habit of being very fond of her grandfather's legal papers. The deer's favorite pastime was to make its way into the grandfather's study always full of all sorts of documents, and to dispose of them in no time. Later on, when the deer was fully grown, the tips of the horns had to be fixed with soft rounds to keep them from harming visitors whom the deer was fond of butting.

Mrs. Gandhi was very kind; it was she who made it possible for me to photograph President Rajendra Prasad's barking deer. The deer was very shy.

En route to Mysore

By plane to Bangalore. The bearer has gone ahead by train. Mrs. B. K. Nehru[1] recommended Mohan Lal, the bearer. Curious coincidence. It turns out I knew Mrs. Nehru as a child. An Hungarian by birth, she was raised in Budapest, and we attended the same school for a year. She showed an old class photograph, and I recognized two of the teachers, and a few of the girls.

Mohan Lal has turned out to be "a find." He speaks, reads and writes English, Hindi, and Urdu; he protects me from beggars, and argues with taxi drivers who always try to overcharge me.

At Hyderabad Airport

Met Luc Bouchage.[2] After a short wait, we board another plane to Bangalore.

[1] Wife of a relative to Prime Minister Nehru.

[2] Friend of Ylla's who designed some of her books.

By car to Mysore

Met at Bangalore airport by Mr. and Mrs. Muthana.[1] Beautiful drive by car to Mysore: lovely, gentle landscape; vegetation very green, and everywhere, ricefields. The cattle here have strange, narrow heads that look like primitive deer-masks. Every time I try to pet one of these gentle looking creatures, they butt me (which is odd, considering they are held to be sacred and are never harmed by anyone).

First days in Mysore

I managed to photograph a suckling elephant and mother on their walk from the Palace stables to a tank in the city. The mother, not used to water, refused to lie down. The baby was very mischievous. Bad light; before the elephants resumed their walk home, it rained.

Trip to Palahalli Island

Went to nearby Palahalli Island in a party consisting of the Muthanas, G. Van Ingen, a Vice Air Marshal, and his brother. The Air Marshal, who is keen on fishing, had hoped for a big catch, but came away with three small fish. His brother tried to shoot a crocodile, a rather small one, seen from time to time basking on a faraway rock. He too had bad luck. Every time he aimed, the crocodile slid into the water, and after a time, did not return to the rock at all.

The boats we took to the island are a very primitive type of water vessel. They look like large, round baskets, and are made of tightly stretched buffalo hide. If treated properly—the hides must be oiled frequently—the boats remain perfectly waterproof. The waters we navigated in these "basket boats" are literally studded with tiny, rocky islands, covered with a great variety of birds: open-billed storks, egrets, cormorants, cranes. These islands constitute a bird sanctuary, a perfect nesting ground—we saw thousands of birds in their nests. As everywhere in India, there was an abundance of

[1] Mr. Muthana, forestry officer of Mysore.

crows here. Most likely they hung around in wait for the parent birds to leave their nests in search of food, and to snatch the babies from their nests while the parents are gone. As we approached the tiny islands, many of the birds flew away in fright, and I fear the crows took advantage of this. There were many open-billed storks, already quite grown, but still not able to fly; they looked comical, perched on the long, thin branches as we passed by. The sky was heavily overcast, and the light was bad for pictures.

First meeting with His Highness of Mysore

Today I was taken in a palace car to meet His Highness. I was brought to the Small Palace where I was first met by His Highness' private secretary who took me through various galleries to a simple drawing room where I was received by His Highness. He was seated below a huge oil painting of one his ancestors. The Maharaja wore a turban, and—in accordance with the current style among Indian men—had a neatly trimmed moustache. At thirty-four, His Highness is rather portly; he speaks carefully, very slowly. We were served tea and coffee. His Highness remarked that Mysore was proud of its coffee. I chose coffee; it was excellent.

On a visit to the soldiers' barracks

Amusing—and touching—incident while visiting the barracks of the Maharaja's soldiers. In the room of one of them, I was greatly amazed to see on a wall covered with Hindu religious pictures and photographs of the Queen of England and Prince Philip, a clipping of one of my photographs that appeared in the British magazine *Illustrated.* Pasted on gold paper, a double-page color picture showing two kittens playing was hung in the middle of the wall as though it had been given the "place of honor." In a camera store the other day, I also came across a print of one of my pictures, this one of a kitten and a dog.

On the children of Mysore

The children here are generally a nuisance. They appear from everywhere, are attracted by the pale skin and dress of Westerners, and in a minute, form a dense wall around their object of curiosity. They all have a special kind of stare: silent, tense, immensely direct. They are fascinated when I change a film or when I use the lightmeter. Lal always tries to chase them off, but they do not go. When I cry in despair: "Lal, Lal, they are in my way. Get them back, get them away!" they repeat my outbursts in a mocking chorus. Lal, poor man, is embarrassed on two counts: he understands all their rude remarks which, fortunately, escape me, and he is put off by my own behavior. No doubt, he thinks I am most undignified. In fact, I am sure I embarrass him every time I jump out from the Palace car and crouch down in the middle of the road to photograph a buffalo or a cow. The driver, used to ambassadors or princes, doesn't approve of this either, and to top it off, I am always in slacks.

Children do some work around elephants. Consequently, I do not find it easy to photograph the elephants in their stables. Before I can get a picture, the children run up and shout: "They are ours. They belong to us!"

Second interview with the Maharaja of Mysore

Today I had a second interview with HH (His Highness). The Dasara has been on now for five day, and I received a call at 10 a.m. that HH wanted to see me. When I reached the Palace, I had to wait a bit in the trophy room. Among the trophies on the walls were the heads of 14 tigers, 6 bears, 10 bison, deer and leopards. HH received me unshaven—not to shave is part of the Dasara ritual. I had to take off my shoes before going into the room where he waited to greet me because he wore a sacred bracelet. The Maharaja was dressed completely in white. A sparrow flew in and out of the room (the sparrow had made a nest in one of the lamps). I remarked on the extraordinary familiarity of animals in India. "They blend in with humans here much better than in any other country," said the Maharaja.

He then showed me his photographs and photographic equipment, which is considerable. He told me he had killed over a hundred tigers. Tiger hunts are carried on in the nearby jungles. He explained that he and his party sit in a machan (a box like an opera loge, situated high up in the trees) during the hunt while beaters drive the tigers, and the drum-beats create a heightened rhythm.

HH showed me pictures of his wife and children, and told me he was, at the moment, hard at work on translating an ancient Sanskrit book on elephants into Hindi.

The Dasara

There is much activity as part of these yearly festivities: theatre, music, folk singing, a parrot circus, etc. The play, two days ago, seemed to me a classical Indian play with costumes, singing and dancing; last night, a modern, realistic play was given, preceded by music and songs of a folk singer. The theatre is free, and it was packed both nights. Men and women do not sit together; everyone was most attentive, and polite.

The parrots gave a fascinating performance. Performing in small cages, some of them were superb acrobats and actors. They guessed cards, picked out numbers which they added and subtracted, pushed little carts, climbed and descended ladders. One parrot performed a very neat trick. He picked up rings about three to five inches in diameter and, lying down and lifting the rings, managed to put his body through them by moving them up and down. Too bad their owner seemed so sullen and utterly without humor.

The ninth day of the Dasara

How glad I am I have come in time to see this remnant of what was once the "fabulous India," the ancient India of true pomp and luxury. Today HH did "puja"[1] to the State elephant, the State horse, the State cow, and to his own cars, horses, elephants and arms, all lavishly decorated: the elephants, horses and cows, painted, bedecked with jewels and cloth; the Rolls Royces and Bentleys covered with precious materials, and garlands of fruit and flowers. All the troops were out, and at attention. The Palace grounds were packed with a most colorful, and well-behaved crowd. Among the fourteen elephants was a baby elephant with white fluff around the ears, playful and very amusing.

[1] Paid his respects by means of religious ritual.

The public is most impressive. The women in colorful saris, squatting as they await the procession, their little children in their arms; and the large groups of young girls, most of them in colorful long dresses, all wearing pigtails and flowers in their hair. The crowd is astonishingly silent and attentive.

The last day of the Dasara

I do not understand the significance of these various customs, but each is ritualistic, and performed with great ceremony. This morning, the Maharaja mounted his riding horse, rode very slowly to the middle of the Palace grounds, descended, and was then carried back to the Palace in a beautiful, all silver palanquin. When he arrived back at the Palace, and left the covered litter, a swarm of bees ascended under the arch where he was expected.

Alas, it poured during the final procession, which did not at all scatter the crowd. Hundreds of people sat in trees, many swinging down from branches. An airplane, flying low, caused a stampede among the bullocks; two were killed and several wounded.

Yesterday, in the club, I heard quite a bit of talk about the leeches during the wet season, and the jungle flies during the dry season, which is not very encouraging for jungle tracking. Meanwhile, it has rained every day, and the grass must be growing steadily. I certainly came here much too early, but am very glad indeed I did not miss the festivities of these last few days.

Hoysala Temples, Mysore

At Sravana Belgola, a man who insisted he was a priest literally glued himself to our steps, talked and talked without stopping. At Halebid Temple, however, a young man belonging to the Archeological Department explained the history of the temple with so much love and enthusiasm I was really delighted to hear him. Flowers—everyone who comes, comes with flowers.

Visit to elephant working camp, Mudumalai Reserve, Mysore

This is the Teppakadu elephant working camp. As it is Sunday, the elephants are not at work but are free to graze in the jungle the entire day. Three of the elephants have babies, six, eight and twelve months old. An expectant elephant mother is put on a big rice and coconut diet; after the baby is born, she does not work for six months (not so much to conserve her strength, but to keep the baby out of the way of the working elephants). The elephants are well looked after: they are scrubbed in the river for an hour in the morning and in the evening, and are fed boiled rice after they have had their bath. At night they graze in the forest.

There is great excitement in the camp. A big tusker lost a tusk in a battle with a rogue. (The tusk, covered with blood, was left lying on the ground.) The tusker is kept within an enclosure through the night to prevent him from seeking out the rogue for revenge.

The baby elephants are putting on some marvelous antics. The oldest one kicks, throws his trunk about, and is generally very fresh; the youngest is practically standing on its head. In the river, they jump all over their mothers and enjoy playing together; they splash, submerge, and really seem to love the water.

To get to the other shore of the river I had to cross on an elephant's back, bare back at that; didn't feel very reassured.

Third visit to His Highness

A third visit with HH at the Summer Palace. First, a game of tennis, then a lengthy film session. Met HH's mother, a shy, charming lady. Unbelievable game of tennis, each ball being chased by a mastiff and a Boston terrier; during the game Dennis Conan Doyle[1] and his wife Nina[2] drive up in a grey Rolls Royce. Later on, HH commented on the films while they were being run. There were three reels on elephants (some excellent scenes of a herd bathing), and one reel on tiger-shooting. The film showing lasted three hours.

[1] Son of the British author.

[2] The Russian Princess Mdivani.

Trip to Bandipur

We met at 9 a.m. at Her Highness' Palace. Her Highness is very fond of birds, keeps an aviary, has four demoiselle cranes in her garden. Some baby peacocks were brought in to be shown to us. His Highness came after an hour, exasperated at having been held up by a government official.

I have to watch my photographic equipment like a hawk. It invariably is put into the wrong car, or is left out in the sun.

The jolting along some of these roads is terrific, much worse than in Africa.

The grass is very high; only saw some deer in the morning.

I very much enjoyed my conversation with HH during lunch. He has a good sense of humor, is very well read and has a keen appreciation for music. Every so often I watched HH's mother, who sat by herself at a separate table. Before the meal began, she took out a little book and read in it; she did so again once the meal was finished (was it a prayer book, I wonder?).

After a lengthy lunch, we resumed our drive again at 4 in the afternoon. Shortly after we started, a huge panther appeared; magnificent beast, stretched out on a tree-trunk. I tried quickly to take a picture, but the panther was gone with the greatest speed. HH was most considerate: the Major, in the front seat, wanted to shoot the panther, but HH held him back so that I might get a picture first. Too bad; I fear I won't have as good an opportunity again.

HH is convinced that snakes will not harm him. He believes in their "subtle force"—HH used these words for lack of a more adequate translation of a Canarese expression.

Elephant hunt

HH arranged an elephant hunt for Conan Doyle. We started out in the morning (in a Daimler), had a snack in a luxurious resthouse, then changed for hunting car, continued for some miles, and then proceeded on elephant-back. The Maharaja, Conan Doyle, and two aides were on the first elephant, a forest ranger, HH's two uncles and I were on the second. The forest was very dense; the party was led by two trackers who walked ahead of the first elephant. We advanced very slowly. In order to be able to move at all the mahout of each elephant had to cut branches with a machete and thereby clear a path. After we advanced in this manner for about twenty minutes, we suddenly stopped. The forest ranger pointed at the thick bush directly ahead of us, and said; "In there. He is in there."

I admit I was scared. If the first shot were to wound the elephant, rather than kill him, the denseness of trees and bushes all around us would make it impossible to retreat quickly, and if our elephants were to battle with the wounded one, we would certainly be swept off their backs by the tree-branches.

I was never afraid in Africa. Although we often approached big herds of elephants, it was always in the plains, and our intentions were always peaceful. But here we had come with the idea of killing.

No doubt HH knew exactly how dangerous the situation was. For although this was to be Conan Doyle's hunt, a volley of shots burst forth from the first elephant. Everyone had aimed, and everyone had fired. But HH was most tactful. I heard him say to Conan Doyle immediately after the shooting: "Congratulations, your first shot killed him."

We advanced through the thick bush; there he lay on his side, the big, beautiful tusker, dead with open eyes.

When we got back to the car—Nina Conan Doyle and HH's mother had followed us in the hunting car—Nina Conan Doyle burst into tears when she was told an elephant had been killed; she said: "Why come to India to kill?"

Indeed, why? I do not understand that need in man to affirm himself heroically by killing. It seems to me that only a creative effort can give one a true sense of fulfillment. Photography fills me with a satisfaction no dead animal could possibly give.

We returned to the lodge where we had a very silent lunch.

At 7 p.m. a report came in of a leopard on a kill. We drove out to Channdi Hill, found the kill but not the leopard. HH did, however, return to the spot at 11 p.m., found the leopard and shot him.

October 27, Mysore Palace

During the evening we listened to a Beethoven sonata, talked of Picasso whom HH likes to his own surprise, although he prefers Landseer or Rembrandt. HH is interested in Freud. We discussed the *Decline and Fall of the Roman Empire,* also Malraux's *Les Voix du Silence,* which the Maharaja had read just recently.

Lunched at Kya Thedevaragudi Lodge, had tea at Budipadage. Beautiful country, the grass very tall; saw a few buffalo, but too much heavy growth in the way to take photos; thick bushes everywhere. The Maharani came along, we went in the Rolls, HH and his mother followed in a smaller car. Later in the day, walking up a hill in the wilderness, we came upon a small, ancient temple located near a pond and a tremendous, old mango tree. A priest came out from the temple bringing a dish filled with flaming oil which was passed among all the members of the royal family; he also presented each with some sort of seeds. Later on, I noticed the entire royal group head for the top of the hill, and I followed. There was a small village and an imposing temple at the top, where to my great embarrassment the royal family had apparently been expected. I felt out of place and wanted to turn back, but they insisted that I stay; all were most polite and did their best to make me feel at ease. I did not enter the temple with the royal family, but could hear the temple musicians playing for them. When they returned, temple food was served on banana leaves. The view was superb, hills and hills, and hills. Monkeys kept appearing right in front of us; unfortunately they were chased away.

I have certainly found Mysore to have the great charm so beautifully expressed in Frances Flaherty's book *Elephant Dance*.

Back at Mysore City, Ellis Dungan [1] telephoned to say he was coming for dinner tomorrow. I cancelled my planned three day trip to Bandipur and went instead to Kanguri to photograph a newborn elephant baby. The baby now stands 3 ft. 2 in., has very large eyes, and a pink, short, rubbery trunk. An elephant baby stands up the first few hours after birth. After that, the baby seldom lies down. This one has trouble finding the mother's nipple; the mother is very calm and dignified. Her diet consists of 10 coconuts and 6 pounds of rice a day.

Driving in India requires great art. When you blow your horn, the person in front of your car never thinks it concerns him, but continues to walk slowly in the middle of the road. Dogs also always lie across the middle of the road, and it is impossible to get them to move; consequently it is the cars that must move around them by circling them; and of course, a cow will never get out of the way; you needn't even bother to blow your horn.

[1] Documentary film maker.

October 30

The royal ladies love the movies; they "live" the picture; they keep on remarking on the fate of the characters; "poor man, how he must suffer"; or "I think she is falling in love," "will they marry?" . . .

Spend an evening with the royal ladies listening to dance records. The Princess dances with a dreamlike expression; Ellis Dungan and I do a waltz, and the ladies are delighted.

November 2, tiger hunt

At last the phone call to inform HH that the tigers have taken the bait. The hunting party is gathered hurriedly: HH, his mother, sister, Conan Doyle and a few others; the party leaves in two Rolls Royces. First to the resthouse for coffee, then by hunting car to the machan (this one consisting of two rows of seats). We are told there are at least three tigers. The beating has started; it is far away, but draws nearer at an even pace, creating an atmosphere of immediacy and tenseness. There are 130 beaters, and 12 shikarees. The tom-tom is even but closer, and the first tiger shoots by like lightning. HH did not fire as it was a small female; she appeared suddenly, very far to the left (I think I got only half of her in the picture). Another tiger now jumps behind a nearby bush where he hides and refuses to come out. The beaters get closer and closer, and the tiger finally does jump out, again way over to the left, but this one is caught in the net, and shot. I thought the hunt was over, but it appeared another tiger was hiding somewhere within the hunting area. The tom-tom starts again; after twenty minutes the third tiger charges across, very far left, very fast, gets hit by HH, but not killed, and speeds away. The shikarees searched the whole afternoon and the entire next day for the wounded tiger. The dead tiger is very beautiful; poor, beautiful thing, with glassy eyes, and soft paws.

The tension worked up during the hour and a half of beating and excited voices was so great it has quite exhausted me. What is the point to all this, really what is the point? The poor, harassed animals! Before they appeared, the bamboos were alive with monkeys and jungle fowl; and then the savage cries and tom-tom of the beaters invading the quiet and dignity of the jungle. Only if we approach animals innocently, only then, it seems to me, can we be fearless and free.

November 9, elephant capture

Very rough ride to the interior of the forest where a hundred pits had been dug, and two elephants captured: a baby tusker, about three years old, in one pit; an elephant mother, about twenty-five years old, in another. The baby was being fed, but not the mother (if she regained her strength she would make it difficult to get her out of the pit). The roping, the first and most important part of the capture, is a delicate undertaking. Under such conditions, elephants are wont to slash out with their trunks and grab the men who have enraged them. The roping is handled by men from surrounding villages who are experts at it (for generations the men of the villages have performed this difficult task). The trapped elephants are wild ones to begin with, but their increased wildness, their rage at having been caught, makes them a frightening sight. The main job in roping the elephant is to secure a large noose around the head. To distract the captured elephant, he is fed sugar cane, and large, tropical leaves are waved at him. Once the rope is tied around the head and leg, large logs are rolled into the pit, which enables the men to pull him out of the pit. Two kunkis (tame, trained elephants) surround the captured one when he comes out of the pit; their presence calms the wild elephant and gives him reassurance. Elaborate precautions are then taken to get the wild elephant to the village where the long training begins. Babies and very young elephants suffer less from stress and shock at being captured than old ones.

Many forest officers are against this method of capture. An elephant caught in a pit will refuse to go near one for the rest of his life; he will lie down near the pit, will roll on the ground, and shriek.

The pits are so well camouflaged I nearly fell into one myself.

The wife of one of the mahouts is constantly following him, always keeping a good distance behind him. It appears they have been married only four months, and she is always there, crouching in the distance, never smiling, never looking at him. He is very good looking, young, has a charming smile, behaves as though he knew she were there but pays her no attention at all.

November 21, dinner at the Van Ingens'

Roasted peacock; it was delicious. Looked like a small turkey, had the same consistency. Before being cooked, is kept in refrigerator for a week, soaked in olive oil, wrapped in cellophane; packed with it is a papaya stem to soften the meat. In Delhi I had also had chicken soaked in papaya juice; the whole chicken is baked in charcoal; very spicy, very delicious, eaten with hand.

November 29, the fifth tiger hunt

Last three hunts were disappointing, a lot of tension, but the tiger retreated each time. Today's hunt was different. The hunting party consisted of HH, Major Singh, two aides-de-camp, Mr. Darasha (HH's secretary); I was the only woman; eighty beaters, a spacious, sunny area in front of the machan. The beating had not lasted more than twenty minutes when tiger growls were heard from behind a bush very near the machan. He did not come out, but it was evident from the rustling among the bushes that he ran way over to the left, about eighty yards away. The bushes were heavy and I did not even catch a glimpse of the tiger, but HH fired and said: "I am certain he is dead." Major Singh was sceptical if the tiger had been hit at all. An order was given to some beaters to get the lorry and drive to the spot where the tiger should be. The lorry was brought, was driven into the bush, and suddenly there was wild cheering: the tiger was dead! Apparently, the beast had dropped instantly. I cannot understand how HH could have shot so accurately under these circumstances; no one had actually seen the tiger running or hiding.

The tiger turned out to be the Maharaja's record, and came very close to India's record. Ten feet seven inches, measured from nose to tail, he weighed six hundred pounds. HH was so pleased and excited, he could not eat his lunch. I was pleased, too, which surprised me, as I am never pleased to see an animal killed. The tiger was very fat, I have never seen one like it even in a zoo. HH told me he had been after this tiger for more than two years. The tiger had been in forty hunts or so, but each time had been clever and cunning. (He had lived entirely on village cattle.) With him in the block today had been two females, but they had left before the beat began. Major Singh believes there must have been a fight about the male.

We drove back to the Palace in a triumphant procession. The tiger was driven in an open car ahead of ours so that the Maharaja's family could have a look at him. The smell of the dead animal was incredible, and the palace dogs were very nervous (the German Shepherd was found hiding under the piano).

November 30, talk with Major Singh on elephants

Was left behind in the machan with Major Singh while HH went off with elephants to look for a tiger he had wounded a week ago. HH did not want the responsibility of having me with him on his elephant when a wounded tiger is in the vicinity, which may mean a battle with the elephant. Had a most interesting talk with Major Singh about elephants.

Baby elephants very often have foster mothers (Elephant Bill[1] calls them "aunties"); usually old females who have not had calves of their own for a very long time. They are very jealous of the babies, and can get more aggressive in defending them than their real mothers. When a baby elephant is born, the herd usually does not move ahead for one to two weeks. During the first day of the last keddah, four babies were born, but each died. They must have been premature due to shock. Four more were born later in the stockade, among them a pair of twins.

HH returned. The tiger was not found.

The tiger HH shot yesterday is "getting" bigger and heavier. The newspaper reports his weight as 900 lbs. (his actual weight was only 600 lbs.).

Some data on working elephants at Kokankote: big tuskers lift logs weighing over a ton, also uproot trees; they work with harness. Logs are loaded in trucks by men, not elephants; the labor of men is cheaper. Working elephants get three months' vacation—June, July, and August; only work four hours a day—otherwise they would not live long.

HH has again a new camera. Almost every day he shows me a new camera, lens or gadget. His technical knowledge is considerable.

December 5

The Minister of Agriculture tells me HH keeps two astrologers in whom he believes firmly. One astrologer told the Maharaja he would have a son after having killed seventy-five. His son is now eighteen months old, and HH's tigers now number 103.

Ila[2] means "no" in Canarese; also "nothing."

[1] Elephant Bill is the name given to the British author, J. H. Williams, after one of his own books.

[2] Pronounced as Ylla's own name.

December 8, sari incident causes much disturbance

I bought a sari, and Lal, the driver and the butler are all very excited when they see me in it. (I wore it yesterday at the Palace; felt rather foolish.) This morning, Lal asked me: "How much did you pay for that sari?"

"Seventy-two rupees," I said.

"That's too much. Fifty would have been right," he said. "You don't know about saris. You should ask someone who knows before buying." He seemed upset.

The word got around, and by now the butler, the driver, even the dhobi (laundryman) have joined Lal, and all seem upset and complain that I paid too much. Lal wanted to go to the shop where the sari was bought to try and get some money back. I wouldn't let him. But he and the others found a way to get even with the shopkeeper. While I was buying something else at a nearby shop, the driver and Lal went to the shop where the sari had been purchased, said the sari had spots in it, and insisted that it be dry cleaned for me.

The Maharani also sent me a sari tonight, with long petticoat and choli (blouse).

December 9, on "prehistoric animals"

Conan Doyle came to see me. He spoke to me about the prehistoric animals described by his father in *The Lost World,* which he believes still exist in Africa, south of the Belgian Congo, in the North Rhodesian swamps. He plans to go with Prince Ali Khan to Ethiopia from where he hopes to pursue the trail. He promised to cable me and give me exclusivity at photographing them.

December 10, on monkeys

A small family of monkeys in the temple hall at Seringapatam. The male, as is his usual custom, keeps the others away. I teased him by not giving him any nuts and feeding the others. He was mad, made faces, and showed he was disgusted with me by yawning at least twenty times. Suresh[1] told me a funny story about an old temple

[1] Suresh Vaidya, Indian journalist.

keeper in New Delhi and some monkeys. It seems the monkeys were particularly mischievous and became such a nuisance to everyone in the neighborhood the municipality decided they had to be caught. An Englishman whom Suresh knows and whose trade it is to trap monkeys and sell them to American laboratories was given permission to catch them. Suresh went along with the Englishman to inform the temple keeper. He was heartbroken. The temple is near the Prime Minister's house, and the keeper said: "Why catch them? They do no harm. Did Nehru complain? No! And why send them to America? What will the Americans do with them? Eat them, of course, what else? Anyway, who are these Americans? Nobody even heard of them three years ago! . . ."

December 14, the Maharaja of Bharatpur and his puja box

I have been assigned a palace tonga instead of the Austin, which was put at the disposal of the Maharaja of Bharatpur, who arrived yesterday.

The Maharaja told me an amusing incident. He was astonished to see the bulk of my equipment and asked me: "How do you manage to keep all your equipment near you on your trips?"

I told him it was quite a problem, since I felt it was necessary never to let my cameras out of my sight.

"I can understand," he said. "But why not follow my example? Whenever I travel, I buy an extra ticket for my puja box (a box containing utensils used in religious rites), and keep the box in the seat right next to mine; although sometimes this creates confusion. Just the other day, I was waiting for the plane to take off at Hyderabad. As usual, I had a ticket for my puja box. It seemed to me the plane was fairly well filled, at any rate we should have left about ten minutes ago, and still we hadn't taken off. So I asked the stewardess what was the matter. 'We are waiting for one more passenger, a Mr. Puja', she said."

Tonight, on my way to the Van Ingens' the horse pulling the tonga would not go beyond the gate, probably because of the smell of hides.[1] In order to avoid a stampede, I left the tonga at the gate.

[1] The Van Ingen brothers own the largest taxidermy establishment in India.

December 15, birthday party for Princess Meenakshi (one of HH's daughters)

The Maharani received the women guests in the large drawing room, the Europeans first, then the Indians; the men sat separately. In their colorful saris, the Indian women looked like gay butterflies next to the mostly very drab-looking white women. In the theatre, sandwiches and pastry were served, both Indian and European style. The Princess and a little white boy were stars of the birthday program which consisted mostly of singing. The royal ladies and HH were seemingly proud of Meenakshi. During the entertainment, the sister of the Maharaja of Bharatpur and I sat directly in back of the Conan Doyles. The sister of the Maharaja of Bharatpur, a noble, classical beauty, is allergic to perfume, and suffered greatly as a result of the perfume cloud surrounding the Conan Doyles. At intermission, the Maharaja's smallest baby was shown and passed among all the guests; at the end of the program beautiful bouquets of flowers were distributed to everyone, including all the men, by the Maharani herself. The entire party had great charm and innocence. The next day the Maharani asked me, rather shyly, how I had liked the program, and her way of serving tea.

December 17, the MB (Maharaja of Bharatpur) and the lady entomologist

Outing with HH, his family, the MB and his retinue. The MB is very lively, has great charm and warmth. He tells about a lady entomologist who specialized in lice; when a tiger was killed for her, she was so grateful to the MB she wanted to name the rare lice found on the tiger after Bharatpur, who declined the honor.

December 18, the MB on astrology, diamonds, and destiny

HH tells of the time when his whole family, including the old nurse, sat in the machan and a wounded tiger climbed up the ladder leading to it and was not killed until he had gotten halfway up the ladder.

The MB holds forth on astrology, diamonds, and destiny. Says there are male and female diamonds, even neuter ones; diamonds can be blue, green or pink. He claims it doesn't matter what jewels a woman wears, it is always only an ornament, but a man wears diamonds for a purpose. Jewelers will lend men several stones which get tried out to see if they bring good or bad luck.

"We princes," he said, "depend entirely on our astrologers, and eighty-five per cent of them are frauds."

He said he could not leave until the tenth, as this was the only auspicious day.

December 20, visit to Muthana

Muthana claims that although elephants are often mean and cowardly in relationship to man, they are most loyal to their own families. Tells of a big tusker who was not caught when his herd was rounded up in a keddah. Some months later, on the day the elephants of his herd were to be auctioned off, he appeared with very sad countenance, let himself be captured, put up absolutely no resistance at being roped, and was auctioned off on the spot for 10,000 rupees, along with the others. Muthana cannot understand how the elephant had known that the herd was leaving.

We fly to Trivandrum early tomorrow. Festive farewells before leaving.

Trivandrum, December 21

Beautiful beach at Kovalam, although full of jellyfish; nice bathhouse, a swarm of boys and young men eager to do something for you, get us lots of coconuts; bought five lobsters for 3 rupees 12 annas.

At Vidyuth, Karamana (a suburb of Trivandrum)

Vidyuth is the name of a boarding house where I am staying. It is run by Wolter Keers, a young Dutchman who has lived in India for five years. The house is on a hill, has a lovely garden; from the roof all one can see is a vast area of palm trees; there are a great number and a variety of birds in the garden and everywhere; Arthur[1] and others are also staying here.

The cook nearly ruined the lobsters. He had taken them out of the shells; I was annoyed, of course, but the lobsters were excellent just the same.

December 22, at a circus in Trivandrum

Went to see a traveling circus with Arthur and Suresh. Not very good, poor imitation of Western type of circus. Audience nearly all men, absolutely spellbound by everything. Suresh volunteers to help in rope-pulling; next to us a man with two very beautiful, well-mannered children turned out to be a prince of the royal house of Travencore; his children's very large eyes seemed almost to extend beyond their temples; general air of amazement and participation pervades the audience.

December 23

Literary conference in Malayalam, Tamil, Canarese, and Sanskrit. As part of the conference there is singing and dancing to entertain participants and visitors. Folk dancing by three sisters, also Katakali[2] and temple dancing; terrific costumes, but poor showmanship—complete neglect of scenery.

The temple in Trivandrum very famous, very orthodox; not only was I not permitted to enter—soldiers guard the entrance—but neither Suresh nor Lal could go in because their torsos were not bare, and they did not wear dhotis (the traditional Indian garment for men).

Everybody here seems extremely alive, intelligent and nice. Was given a State car, very good-looking driver who is always silent (he always wears a beautiful, white uniform, speaks neither English nor Hindi).

Beautiful drive to Cape Comerin; stayed at guesthouse, very large pool, meals served by the sea.

[1] Arthur Gregor, American poet.

[2] Ancient Hindu dance-drama.

December 25

I went to see a doctor (I have had a nasty skin irritation) who refused to look directly at me, and who was most embarrassed when I asked him to examine the spots on my thighs—the irritation had spread all over. Nevertheless, although he scarcely examined me, he promises a complete cure within two days.

December 27

The itching is getting worse despite the doctor's assurances.

Everyone at Vidyuth has gone to a famous astrologer in a nearby village; retained by one or two wealthy Trivandrum families, he is supposed to be very good. Arthur suggested that I go along with them, but I refused. If something terrible is supposed to happen to me, I would rather not know beforehand.

January 2, 1955, Aranya Nivas, Periyar Lake Reserve

The rooms in this hotel are very dark, and the light is not turned on until six in the evening. I found no hangers, and when I asked for some, I was told that the hotel is run by the State government, and that there had been no orders to put hangers in the rooms. Mr. John, the hotel manager, a very short young man with green eyes, was very hurt because I had complained.

He burst out: "You have hurt me deeply. I am a government employee, but I always try to do my best. We are in the wilderness here, twenty people who sacrifice their lives to make this hotel run."

Poor Mr. John, he almost broke out into tears, and I had to console him. He was absolutely sincere about all this, and although the whole matter seemed absurd, I found his attitude extremely touching.

Periyar Lake

Periyar Lake is an artificial lake that consists of many small lakes and connected canals. There is a huge dam, the trees in the flooded area have not been cut, and dead trees and branches, looking like tortured ghosts imploring heaven to free them, are emerging everywhere and make navigation rather difficult and hazardous. The lakes are surrounded by a chain of hills, some thickly forested, others covered by high grass. All very beautiful, very romantic.

The whole area is a wild life reserve, one of the oldest in India; shooting has been prohibited for twenty years. We have been navigating in a motor launch. Few animals can be seen, they are shy and head for the interior when they hear the motor noise, which is really deafening. Usually the motor is turned off when we approach a region where animals are likely to graze at the edges or bathe. Sometimes we take a few steps inland, but can't go far: the forests are thick and impenetrable. It is obvious from droppings and footprints that there are many elephants here. One can even smell them and hear them breaking and crunching the branches. There are also bison and sambars.

Yesterday we saw a sambar stag grazing near the water's edge, his back turned toward us. The female, hidden behind some trees, alerted him, and like a flash, he sped away, then turned around toward us, his body partly hidden by a bush, his head emerging partly, his horns blending with the branches of the trees. From time to time he barked angrily and seemed to challenge us to a fight. We passed him in the boat, and he continued to bark as we passed.

I start out every morning at six. It is still dark, and I watch the sun rising slowly over the hills. It takes about ninety minutes to reach the parts of the reserve where animals are most likely to be found. I have been hoping to catch an elephant herd at bath in the morning, but have had no luck so far. We did see some elephants yesterday. They were grazing near the water, and we managed to get quite close to them, but as soon as they became aware of us they ran away, their tails lifted high.

My guide here is Mr. Wood, a retired game ranger. He is sixty-five, toothless, very much alive, agile like a hare, I can hardly keep up with him. He has been here for thirty years and knows every corner in this game sanctuary.

Few wading birds are to be seen, some white herons.

Finally, at long last, I was able to get some pictures of elephants, but I am worried about movement; I had to take the pictures from the swaying boat, and the tripod was of little help.

In the evening, I hear an elephant herd bathing somewhere near the hotel, but although there is a full moon, I cannot see a single animal. I can hear them splashing, and from time to time, trumpeting.

January 5, Periyar Lake

Strange medical service provided by the hotel: If you don't feel well you write your symptoms on a piece of paper which is taken by a bearer on bicycle to a doctor who lives about a mile from here. After a while, the bearer returns with the medicine—both "consultation" and medicine are part of the hotel service and are free.

Looked over the classified advertisements in "The Hindu." Astrology is classified under professional heading. The marriage ads—there are many—are written by and addressed to parents. The girl's skin is usually given first (fair, very light, etc.), then follows her education; looks, dowry and expectations are also mentioned; horoscope is always asked—many times the caste is stated ahead of all other qualifications.

A woman's "privacy" is rather a problem on these boat trips. When I propose that we land so that I may disappear behind a tree, Wood says: "What do you want to go behind a tree for? There is nothing to photograph there."

I have to insist energetically that in spite of this fact I want to go behind a tree, and only then does the meaning dawn on him.

Saw a flock of yellow-black hornbills in a heavy flight, with spread tails; the noise of our motor startled them, and they suddenly arose from a huge fig tree; also saw Malabar squirrels, and huge, black monkeys with little spots of grey on top of their heads.

We leave for Trivandrum for a day or two; from there to Bombay.

Trivandrum

It is impossible to get fresh cut flowers, but the bazaar is full of stands where flowers are stripped of petals and leaves, and with fruit—mostly limes—are rearranged into long garlands or bouquets that look as though they were taken out of a primitive painting.

At the airport, Arthur brought us garlands made of rose petals, jasmine, and lime.

Bombay, middle of January

Very good shopping. Saw Ellis Dungan who advised me to go directly to Assam where five pits are now being dug to capture a rhino for the Philadelphia zoo; also keddahs are being prepared there. I was tempted to cancel my trip to Saurashtra, but did not want to get into disfavor with the Saurashtra government. I wired Stacey instead and asked him to hold up the pit digging until my arrival in Assam. A wire arrived from Jim Burke[1] confirming a *Sports Illustrated* assignment. I am to meet John Huston, the movie director, in Calcutta on the 29th (January) and join his tigerhunt party.

January 17, Gir Forest, Saurashtra

I have come to Saurashtra as a guest of State, and was received most cordially. The Gir Forest is one of the few lion reserves left in India, and the people in the surrounding villages are proud of the forest.

The cattle on the way up here were very beautiful: majestic, heavy, white, with crowns of heavy horns (quite different from the deer-like, light Mysore cattle). The villages are very colorful: women dressed in red, brown, rust-colored shawls, and mirror-embroidered skirts; blouses are bare in back, consist of a sort of brassière; women wear heavy silver jewelry. The people use beautiful brassware for carrying water. The villagers like to be photographed, pose well, and are generally very good looking.

Although the lions feed mainly on tame buffalo—the villagers near the forest have only herds of buffalo, not cattle—the villagers take pride in their lions. There is a superstition here that if the lions were to leave this vicinity, the buffalo would cease to give milk; and also that if a cow is attacked by a lion but survives, she ceases to conceive.

January 20, Gir Forest

Lions are much bolder at dusk and in the dark than during the day. This morning we came across four lions, but I was only able to photograph one, the rest disappeared quickly behind a thick bush.

[1] James Burke, of the New Delhi Bureau of TIME, Inc.

Nilgai—the large antelopes of India—look like giraffes in these parts. What makes them look so large is the smallness of the thorny trees, which must be some kind of acacia; these, the burnt yellow grass, the wide open spaces are reminiscent of the African plains.

In this part of India buffalo are not used as oxen; an old buffalo cow is used to carry water. Yesterday I noticed a cow in a herd with large wounds on her back. I was told they had been inflicted by a lion about a month ago; the cow had been attacked but rescued by the herd. Buffalo have an excellent herd instinct. It is usually at dusk, when returning home, that the last buffalo in a herd is attacked and killed by a lion.

Coming home, I saw two lionesses and three cubs on the road.

January 24, Gir Forest

Left early this morning to look for nilgai; very near a village spotted a lioness and her three-month-old cub. Near the road lay the kill: a big buffalo cow, belly open, intestines and tail already disposed of. We drove away and returned several times hoping the lions would return to the kill, but they lay not far from the kill, half hidden in a bush, and would not come out, no doubt waiting for us to leave.

On the road, we met several ox-carts and peasants on foot, and warned them of the lions ahead. A detour would be safest, we told them. But lions here are very much part of the life of the villagers. The peasants armed themselves with sticks and stones, thanked us, but proceeded. All the villages around here are surrounded by thorny hedges to keep the lions out, and the fields are protected from the greedy nilgai by stone walls.

I leave in a day or two. Compared to a big game hunter, the requirements of a photographer are so much more involved and exacting. I feel the entire forest staff—trackers and officers—are exasperated with me.

February 5, on tiger hunt in Cooch Behar with John Huston

Five days have passed and no tiger has been shot, the mood in the camp has been gloomy. When, at long last a tiger did appear, John Huston as well as F.F.

(F. D. Fenston of London) missed him, and I could not get a picture. Huston's elephant has been very unsteady, shies excessively; consequently we changed elephants. I was sorry about this as my elephant's name was Ila Devi—goddess Ila.

This hunt, though spectacular—a great many elephants are taking part in it—is very difficult to photograph. I have to work entirely from elephant back. In the beginning, the daily ride, which lasts from four to seven hours, made me feel stiff and aching, but I have gotten used to it by now and can take it quite well.

The elephants are equipped according to the service they must perform. For great distances we ride on "pads"—mattresses like saddles—while during the actual shoot elephants with "howdahs" (high wooden box saddles) are ridden. Very often we change during the day from one to another.

To take pictures from elephant back is very difficult because the animal is never really steady, and also because it is difficult to communicate with the mahout, who speaks no English. I have missed a great many pictures because the mahout does not follow orders fast enough—my orders are being translated by an Indian who is also on my elephant.

There are two types of beats: a general beat when all elephants, including those carrying shooters, form a straight line and advance through the jungle hoping to beat out any game hidden in it; the other is the more spectacular beat. And that occurs when a tiger having killed a bait is lying in a known area. Then the four howdah elephants—which includes mine—are placed in a line at about sixty to eighty feet apart, and the eighteen remaining elephants beat the tiger toward the shooters.

February 6, on tiger hunt with John Huston

During the shooting I am usually placed on the edge, but today I was put between two shooters.

At first a leopard was shot. Being wounded, he attacked the beating elephants and mauled the trunk of one. This happened in high grass, and I could not see it at all. Suddenly, the wounded leopard broke out of the bush in front of my elephant. I could certainly have gotten him this time, but my elephant, greatly frightened, bolted.

I have been sick for a day and a night. It is very cold here at night and my allergy is at its worst.

Was given two injections which helped considerably.

There is an open fire before the camp. It makes a marvelous picture and creates all the atmosphere one reads about, or imagines when thinking about hunts in exotic places. Some of the men stay up till three in the morning, sitting around the fire, talking in hushed voices; occasional laughter...

Captain Singh entertains us with the story of his second marriage—sounds like the fastest Hindu marriage in history.

February 7

This morning we received the usual news: no kill was spotted. Nevertheless, a beat was ordered and a tiger was in fact beaten out.

In the afternoon, the procedure was repeated. A kill had not been spotted, but we were all ordered on a random beat. Everybody considered the beat more or less hopeless.

We were advancing in one line in an open field of high grass, when someone behind me shouted: "Tiger!" I saw a tiger dashing by on my right with fantastic speed. So sudden was his emergence, and so quickly did the whole thing happen, I didn't even see the second tiger who, I was later told, had run by on my left. Huston aimed, shot, and—we later discovered—killed one of the tigers. (It seems we had disturbed two full-grown cubs who had just left their mother.) Huston's shot was excellent; he had been unprepared and aimed at the tiger from a great distance. He was radiant; the general tension was relieved.

The beat was continued; again a tiger ran across, too distant for pictures; F.F. shot and wounded the tiger. The animal kept hidden in the grass and growled furiously. The elephants were so frightened they had to be driven to advance and form a circle around the wounded tiger. Great confusion followed, but F.F., shooting again, killed the tiger.

February 8

A kill was announced. This meant we knew where the tiger was, and we set out in a truck; the elephants had been sent ahead. When we arrived, it was most impressive to see all the elephants waiting in a group. Far in the distance, the tiger appeared; F.F. took the shot, and got the tiger. A magnificent beast, ten feet long, 495 pounds in weight. The tiger was skinned, the villagers took the meat they wanted, and the feast of the vultures started: grim, macabre, surrealistic—the movements of the vultures, of their wings and jaws; the tiger picked clean in no time; a stray dog fighting off the vultures for some prey.

February 11, the last day of the hunt

General beat through a forest that bore all the aspects of a forest in a fairy tale: light green ferns, a gentle play of light, a dreamlike reality... Not a single animal... Home by 3 p.m.

February 12

150-mile drive by jeep to Cooch Behar Palace, about sixty years old, Italian architecture; dinner terribly late.

February 15, Kaziranga wild life sanctuary, Assam

Upon my arrival at Jorhat, I was met by Mr. E. P. Gee, manager of Doyang Tea Estate at Oating. Mr. Gee, who is most hospitable, had done his best to see that I am comfortable here. Went to a large party, met a great number of tea planters. Visited tea gardens and plantations. Met Mr. P. D. Stacey, Chief Conservator, a friend of Dorothy Flaherty, a man of great charm and dynamism. We had had a long correspondence, and I was glad to meet him at last.

February 16, in the sanctuary

Thanks to Stacey the rhino capture was postponed until my arrival. The Philadelphia zoo bought a young female rhino two years ago, and now they ordered a young male. For that reason everything was arranged, pits were dug, and elephants were kept ready to drive rhinos toward the pits during the following night, the safest time for bringing in a captured rhino. However, this morning a report came that a rhino had fallen into one of the pits. The ranger, Mr. Das, went out to the pit, and I went with him to watch the capture—the rhino has to be roped and moved into a cage.

Roping a rhino is complicated, but getting him into the cage is a very complex and strenuous job. This difficulty was increased by the fact that the cage took a long time to arrive at the pit, it was very hot and the rhino suffered from the exposure to the sun. By the time the cage was brought it was noon, and the rhino, no doubt exhausted not only from the heat but his resistance to capture, collapsed while being pulled into the cage, and died. Mr. Das was terribly upset.

February 23, Kaziranga sanctuary

I must admit, I feel apprehensive on my elephant's back when a rhino threatens to charge. I do not press forward then. I am not sure I could keep on the elephant's back when he bolts. Sometimes a rhino—stirred out of his mudhole by the noise of the approaching elephants—watches us come closer with a most menacing expression. Undecided whether they should charge or not, rhinos often turn around and bolt.

The early morning drives are very lovely. We are usually out in time to see the sun rise, a huge red ball that dispels the mist, low over the plains. It is cool when the day begins, but the rising sun feels gentle and warm. There are many birds—mostly of the stork and crane family—looking fragile and mysterious in the rising mist.

February 25, photographing rhinos from a "hideout"

Since rhinos are so easily frightened off, I decided to try my luck today by making use of Ellis Dungan's hideout, which is a kind of machan made of hides, a most makeshift contraption, absolutely no protection against a bad-tempered rhino. But I got into the hideout, crouched there hoping to be able to photograph some rhinos; Das and his three elephants were supposed to round them up and drive them past me. And they did. One rhino was particularly obliging, stopped directly in front of my hideout, quietly looked around, then wandered off. I signalled to have the whole process repeated, and the rhino did reappear three or four times. At one point, he was no more than two feet away from me, which was a most thrilling experience.

Deeper in the sanctuary, looking for mothers and babies, we came upon a cow with a two-year-old calf, who both stared at us and, surprisingly enough, did not move away. But bad luck: at that moment my 150 mm. lens gave out; also noticed to my dismay that I had run out of black and white film, so I had to work in color with my 300 mm. lens; Akbar, my temperamental elephant, kept flapping his huge ears; all of which was most distracting. The baby rhino went into the bush, came out again and stood near its mother, but with the 300 mm. lens I could only get one rhino into the view-finder. Going on a bit, we came again upon "mother and child"—the mother relaxing in a mudhole and the baby standing nearby. But again the long lens was a handicap; it was maddening. For once I am lucky enough to sight two rhinos who practically pose for me, and my equipment gives out!

I also developed quite a backache from having crouched so long in E.D.'s contraption.

The forest is indeed a jungle: dense, forbidding, hostile, covered with undergrowth, damp, swampy, full of leeches, creepers on every tree.

March 7, Benares, in monkey temple

Monkeys everywhere. Completely unpredictable. One approaches me quietly for peanuts, which I give him, but suddenly, for no good reason, he starts yelling and all the monkeys scatter. A little beggar boy comes in to tell me one of the monkeys has snatched away one of my shoes which I left at the door. Lots of children gather and, led by the beggar boy, a chase begins. The monkey is chased everywhere, on the roof, up and down, in and out of rooms and yards. Finally they catch him and bring me the shoe triumphantly. I had already resigned myself to driving back to the hotel for another pair of shoes. A few minutes later, a monkey steals the shawl from a woman just as she enters the temple. The monkey runs with the stolen shawl, and the rest of the monkeys, apparently thinking that all this is hilariously funny, become very excited. The woman seems quite accustomed to their tricks and makes no attempt to recover the shawl. A man enters, lifts his hands toward heaven, salutes the goddess, and pays not the least attention to the monkey-commotion about him.

Was taken by a guide to a Nepalese love temple where an old priest points to the realistic love scenes engraved in wood and stone panels throughout the temple.

The cows in Benares appear even more independent than elsewhere; they just about seem to "tolerate" humans. The streets are also full of very tough, immense goat bucks.

Many, many different types of people in the streets, in the doorways, on temple steps; many sadhus (monks).

A beggar woman, old, sick, toothless, playing with a one-year-old infant, who bears an enchanted, pleased expression.

Nowhere else in India have I been as aware of the tremendous difference between the rich and the poor as in Benares. Rich and pompous gold brocades are on sale everywhere—sumptuous materials woven in dark, airless rooms, by workers who receive next to nothing for their labor.

March 8, Benares, monkey temple and silk market

I returned to the monkey temple. The monkey "goings-on" were more or less the same as yesterday. I didn't realize when I came here the first time how colorful is the display of the flower vendors in front of the temple.

They certainly are mischievous, these monkeys. They push people just for the fun of it, jump on people's backs, tear at their flowers. It seems they once grabbed 2000 rupees from a worshipping gentleman, and from the rooftop scattered the hundred-rupee notes all over the street.

Dogs do not treat the temple monkeys as good naturedly as do people. One dog started a fight with a monkey; first the dog chased the monkey away, but soon a whole group of monkeys returned to the scene of the fight in no time at all.

I visited the Benares silk market: in crooked, narrow streets the silk merchants sit under an archway on white pads. No merchandise is on display. Upon request, the merchant runs into his shop and returns with a variety of silks.

In the afternoon, I visited the brass market, and then the Golden Temple.

March 9, on the Ganges

Morning boat ride on the Ganges. People bathing, saying their prayers, washing their clothes, doing exercises; pigeons sitting on bamboo rafts in the river; a corpse clad in red ready for burning; cows standing at the river's edge drinking, walking away, dogs playing—a strange world, impenetrable, immensely peaceful.

March 10, breakfast with Mr. Nehru and his daughter in New Delhi

Also in the breakfast party was a manager of Tata (vast industrial firm), two Parsi ladies with short, white hair, and two little girls. Nehru's daughter wore a green choli (blouse) with a green and white Cottage Industry sari. Before breakfast I had a talk with her about animals and animal conservation in India. When the others arrived, Indira suggested we start breakfast ahead of her father, who eats so quickly he would catch up with us at any rate. However, a few minutes later Nehru arrived and we all sat down to breakfast together. Nehru was most affectionate with the children, but I believe he was a bit put off by my presence; he probably was looking forward to a quiet breakfast with just close friends and family. Nevertheless, it was actually he who was responsible for my presence; he had insisted on being present when I photographed the pandas. Bhimsa, the male, is at his best when Nehru is around.

The pandas are absolutely charming.

Tashi, the female, is prettier and bigger, but extremely shy. They are in a large cage that can be entered. They are fond of peas in husks, which they eat out of their feeder's hand. When he feeds them, Nehru wears white gloves to avoid being scratched. They are away in the mountains for six months—to escape the heat; the rest of the time they spend in an enclosure on the Nehru grounds.

As soon as they were let free they climbed the tree around which their cage is built, and refused to come down. I was told later on it wasn't until after lunch that they finally came down and went back into the cage.

Nehru has great charm. He is handsome and looks younger than his age.

Breakfast consisted of porridge, scrambled eggs on toast. The first Alphonso mangoes of the season were on the table, along with peeled white almonds and large seedless raisins. Maple syrup was served with the porridge. (Mrs. Eleanor Roosevelt sends a bottle of syrup each Christmas.)

March 20, Bharatpur

The Maharaja of Bharatpur is certainly one of the nicest and most charming men I have ever met, completely disarming and most cordial. He told me that he is keeping a full year's mourning for his wife—only thirteen days are customary for a deceased woman. Contrary to other men in his position, he uses no perfume, eats only certain foods, and only attends very special functions.

His wife, who died at twenty-seven, was only fourteen when he married her. Some people say that she "let herself die" after having given birth to a fifth daughter, out of fear that he would take another wife who might give him a son. The Maharaja seems to mourn her very sincerely, without pose or false sentimentality, but—one feels—with articulate grief.

A swim in the pool after the hot drive in the Bentley was most refreshing.

The Maharaja wears two strings of gold and stones around his neck, a large diamond on one finger, and an amethyst cut in the shape of a ram's head on another. He is deeply religious, spends an hour and a half each morning in worship, and uses roses during his puja.

On the way here, the M. pointed out to me the royal family's ancestral tombs. Ceilings of each tomb are covered with enchanting paintings of a Sultan's summer palace, battles, scenes from the life of Krishna.

A buffet dinner was served on the lawn, attended by about twenty or so men who all sat in a half circle, far away from me. Two orchestras entertained.

March 21, dinner on the roof-gardens of the Palace

A most romantic spectacle.

The roof-gardens had originally been laid out for the M.'s grandmother, who was in purdah, and who wished to take her walks in total seclusion. Now a round baldachin-covered structure in the middle of the roof serves for reclining—a great many colorful cushions are heaped on the floor. On the balcony above, a singer performed accompanied by an orchestra; the indirect lighting was very soft, and we were served on very low, separate tables. The M. wore wide white Indian trousers, an emerald green shirt, and a brocaded vest.

The M. is very fond of brocades and other rich materials which he keeps stored in great quantity. Some of the precious textiles can be melted and rewoven.

The M. has a warmth and simplicity that are most endearing.

When I wanted to photograph some deer in the forest, he said: "Do not disturb the deer."

I said with surprise: "But the government has given me permission to photograph them."

"Yes," he answered, "but do, please, take your photographs from a considerable distance, so they will not be disturbed."

"The deer will hardly be seen that way," I pleaded.

"Do not disturb them," he insisted.

"Couldn't we make them run?" I asked. "We don't want to see them only in a standing pose."

"The government orders that they not be disturbed," he replied.

"What is the activity of most deer in the forest?" I asked, hoping to get him around to see my point.

"They graze," he said, "and rest in the shade."

"Do they not sometimes run?" I probed further.

"Yes, they do run."

"Do they die as the result of it?"

"No," he said, "they do not die."

"Then why should it be bad for them to run? Exercise will do them good. Aren't men stronger and healthier when they exercise?"

"Yes, they are," he said. "All right, you may go ahead."

March 23, The Palace at Bharatpur

It is evident from the arrangement of the various quarters in this palace that, though the women were at one time withdrawn from nearly all the activities of their men, they were nonetheless forever present. If the royal ladies were barred participation, they could certainly always watch from behind latticed walls and windows, could hear and see exactly what was happening in the rooms where the men gathered, without ever leaving their own quarters. In a way, silently present at all times as they seem to have been, one gets the impression that these ladies knew much more about their men than the men about their women. The men, it certainly appears, must have always been watched, if not judged.

Week-end, March 26, 27

The Maharaja with sixteen of his guests drove to one of his palaces about an hour's drive from here. A truckload of servants had left ahead of us. In the afternoon a tiger hunt was arranged.

Three machans were set up, two shooters were placed in each. The M., some other guests and I watched the hunt from an observation tower. Fifty beaters drove out one tiger, who was wounded, growled furiously, retreated to a bush, and was found dead the next day.

In the evening, a buffet on the lawn of the palace; again an orchestra and a singer.

Next day, we went out on the lake in two motor launches on a wild geese hunt, while along the shore a beat was arranged for partridges. M. hoped to shoot eighty; actually only six geese were shot and twenty partridges.

The Palace is on a hill overlooking the lake; lovely view.

A panther hunt in the afternoon. We watched from a machan set up fifty feet from the bait. By 6:30 it was too dark for pictures, even with a Tri X. Shortly after 6:30 a panther was spotted, but he had seen us and did not come out. A hyena comes by; night falls; the birds retire with a farewell of great, though melodious noise, and we leave at 7:45. The peace and serenity cannot be described.

The next day, the Maharaja asked me: "What do you think of my guests? I like to discuss them. When you leave, we will discuss you too."

March 28, the Fair at Bharatpur

Incredible atmosphere of festivity, charged with excitement and joy. Upon arrival, we are taken up to the roof of a building from which we watch this joyous spectacle:

The many dancers, the bullocks decorated in all bright colors, the women dressed in orange, shy and hiding their faces; the ferris-wheel merry-go-round turned by a man, and the crowd spotting the Maharaja cannot be controlled, and cheers and cheers . . .

Painted elephants lined up by mahouts in Palace courtyard each morning of the festival (left). Elephants and carriages arranged in front of Palace (Temple in background) ready to receive "puja" on next-to-last day of the Dasara (right).

The festival of Dasara has been celebrated in Mysore since time immemorial. Founded on an ancient legend, the "Feast of Nine Nights and the Tenth Day" honors a hero's victory over a monster. The festivities are marked by religious ceremonies presided over by the Maharaja of Mysore, and are highlighted by processions on the Palace grounds in which the State Horse and the State Elephant play important parts. Second in rank to the State Elephant is the Howdah Elephant (page 45). One of the oldest tuskers in the Royal stables, he carries the Maharaja during the procession on the last day of Dasara. During the entire festival the elephant is elaborately decorated—he is painted, hung with ornaments, and the sawn-off ends of his tusks are replaced by points of gilded metal.

Before each ceremony during the Dasara, the elephants are painted in the Royal stables. Special artists apply picture motifs to the trunk, head, ears, legs and tail of every participating elephant. Following each ceremony, the decorations are washed off.

A wild tusker trumpeting in the jungles of Mysore. Approaching a camp of working elephants, he will at times engage a tame tusker in a fierce fight that often does not end until one of the animals has lost a tusk in the fighting.

Whether wild or tame, elephants have great loyalty to their herds. In Mysore the story is told that a wild tusker not caught when his herd was rounded up in a keddah appeared mysteriously some months later on the very day that his herd was auctioned off. Putting up no resistance at all, he let himself be captured, and was auctioned off along with the herd.

Two mahouts engage their tuskers in a mock battle. They cannot permit the big animals to spar with one another too long or the fight becomes too serious.

At Kokankote—an elephant working camp in Mysore—big tuskers wear harnesses to uproot trees and lift logs that often weigh more than a ton. The working elephants are well looked after. Attendants scrub them in the river for an hour in the morning and in the evening. Their diet consists of boiled rice and grazing in the forest at night. Elephants work only four hours a day, are on vacation for three months of the year; this is done to conserve their strength.

In the wild Mysore forest a baby elephant and its mother wander off from a herd for a while. While she grazes, the 300-pound youngster rests or nurses from her. The mother is a strict disciplinarian and does not let the baby wander far from her side for fear of tigers, which are the little one's worst enemy. If not obeyed she uses her trunk to spank the young one, much to its squealing discomfort. And when on the move with the rest of the herd, she pushes the baby along before her by means of her trunk. Ordinarily the baby elephant stays with its mother until it is at least three or four years old. A mother in a working camp is taken off her work for six months after having given birth. This is done not so much because she needs a rest, but because the baby would be in the way of the other elephants.

A tiger hunt in the vast plains of Cooch Behar or Assam is a spectacular affair, in which sometimes as many as twenty-six elephants participate. In one type of beat all elephants, including those of the shooters, advance in one line to beat out any game that may be hidden in the high grass. When a tiger is known to have killed his bait, the elephants carrying the shooters—the howdah elephants—are placed 60 to 80 feet apart, while the rest of the elephants drive the tigers toward the shooters. Once a tiger is killed, all the elephants converge on him.

The Bengal tiger is an animal of the dense jungle—a beautiful but dangerous animal which lives and hunts alone throughout the year, except for a few brief weeks during the mating season. Although tigers will lie in ambush for the small wild animals of the forest, they often become the scourge of the farmers as well, carrying off their sheep, calves and even cows.

Although the tiger is a good climber, he prefers the forest ground where he can lurk in the foliage and deep underbrush, his striped body partially camouflaged by the filtered light. Unlike most members of the cat family, who are fearful of water the tiger likes water and is a good swimmer.

India was once well populated with lions but today there are probably less than three hundred left. They are all in the Gir Forest, an area of about 480 square miles north of Bombay, which has been declared a wildlife sanctuary to save the Indian lion from complete extinction. Since there are villages within the forest, the inhabitants do occasionally suffer the loss of a cow, but on the whole they are proud of their lions. They believe their buffalo cows would cease to give milk if the lion should ever completely disappear. A social animal, lions live in family groups or prides; not only do these prides share food among themselves, but in securing that food they will often hunt cooperatively.

A leopard lurks on the limb of a tree.

The leopard is smaller than either the lion or tiger but quite their equal in fighting and is the most savage and treacherous of the three. A wary hunter, he will lie in ambush on branches overhanging game tracks used by antelope and other animals on their way to water. Once he kills, the leopard will often drag his prey back up that same tree, where he can devour his meal in quiet. Normally he will not attack man, but will retreat if possible. When provoked or wounded, the leopard will turn and fight savagely.

The Kaziranga Sanctuary in Assam shelters most of India's rhinos. For years hunted by natives for their 24-inch horns and other parts of the body which were believed to have aphrodisiac and medicinal qualities, they had become virtually extinct a few decades ago. Due to government protection their number is on the increase again. Today there are about 250 of the huge rhinos in the Sanctuary, which can be penetrated by visitors on elephantback. Rhinos are not usually aggressive, but occasionally a protective mother or a young male will come lumbering out of the tall grass with his short tail held straight up as he charges right for the intruding visitor.

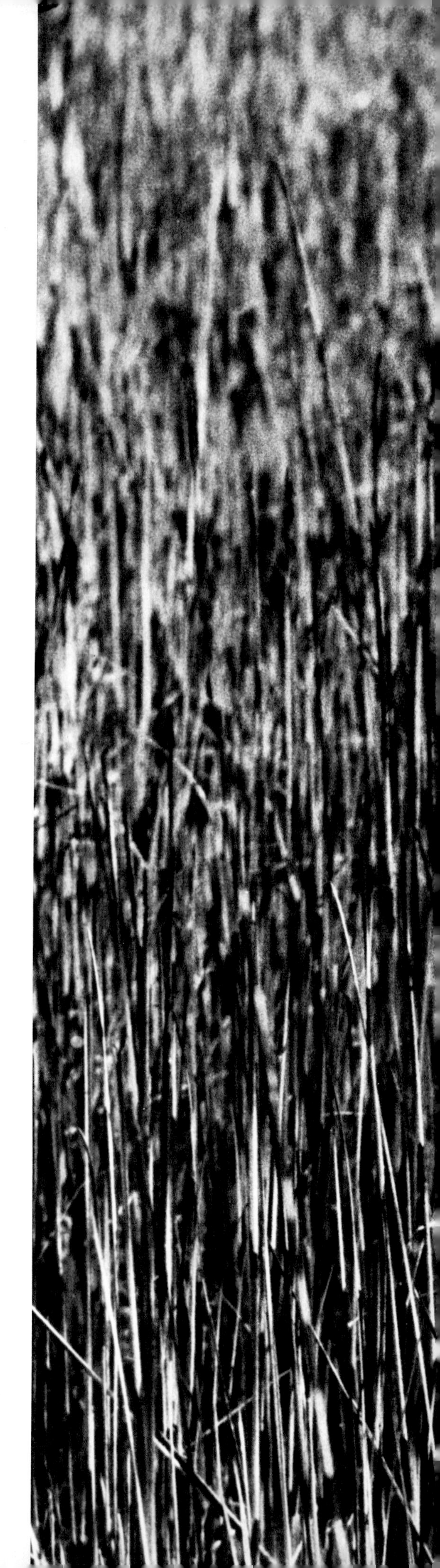

The Indian rhino is protected by his own great strength, thick, overlapping folds of skin that give him an armorplated look and a sharp sense of smell, but has only fair hearing and very poor eyesight. A unique relationship exists between the rhino and the small tick bird or oxpecker. These small birds swarm over the backs of large game animals removing the ticks they find there. Always alert and keen-eyed, the little guests give warning to the rhino at the least disturbance.

Colonies of black-headed ibis are located among the Palahalli Islands in Mysore. A native bird of India, hundreds can be found building their large, stick nests in the tangled tree branches near the water's edge in the spring and summer breeding season.

Water birds of all kinds are found along the shores of the Palahalli Islands. Resting on a branch (above) are a cormorant, open-billed stork, Indian house crow and black-headed ibis.
To the right: storks nesting.

A flight of geese passes overhead (pages 80/81).

The long-legged cranes—demoiselle left, sarus right—are common near water in Assam and elsewhere in northern India.

A flock of painted storks on the edge of a shallow marsh, where they will wade through muddy water with their bills partially open ready to seize fish, eels, frogs or crabs. Like other storks they are noted for their habit of clattering their mandibles

together and shaking their heads from side to side. Soon after the monsoons, they nest in huge colonies alongside other social birds such as spoonbills, herons and egrets.

Vultures are usually seen either bickering among themselves as they fight over food or roosting quietly in a tree digesting their meal. A bedraggled-looking bird with characteristically naked head and neck, it has weak claws and usually feeds exclusively on carrion and garbage.

When vultures get hungry they take to the air and patrol large areas searching for food. They soar slowly in wide circles, ready to swoop down. When a carcass is spotted, one vulture descends after another until there are twenty or thirty clustered around an animal such as the tiger (right). There is a great jostling for position and in very little time the bones are picked clean; while the big birds are so heavily gorged they cannot take to flight.

An extraordinary familiarity exists in India between animals and the people of the towns and villages, who treat them—a cow walking along a main street, a peacock strutting about the pavement—as if they were part of their community.

सुख
लि. मथुरा

The intelligent and appealing rhesus monkey, called bandar by the natives, is the common monkey of India. Troops of them frequently take up residence in the temples where the priests and people bring them food.

The long-tailed, long-furred monkeys known as langurs are considered sacred by the Hindus. They are noted for carrying their tails in graceful curves over their backs, but in spite of their wistful expressions they are aggressive, tough fighters when they get into a quarrel. Female langurs are devoted mothers and carry their young clasped to their bellies for many months.

A young langur pensively eats some fruit (left). Below, an adult rhesus rests against an old tree stump.

The rhesus mother takes good care of her offspring. When small she carries it clutched to her belly, but when bigger and stronger the baby hangs on piggy-back style. Unlike many other species of monkey, the rhesus does not mind water and is a good swimmer.

Wanderoos are called lion-tailed monkeys because, like lions, they have tufts on the end of their tails. Above, a young wanderoo; to the right, an adult with the huge ruff typical of the species.

Hoolock gibbons are tailless apes highly adapted to life in the trees. Possessing greatly elongated forearms, they swing from tree to tree by brachiation (hand over hand), only using their feet to carry food. When they feed they often hang by one arm, using the other to gather up fruit, leaves or insects. Unable to swim and fearful of water, they dip their hands in water and suck their fingers when they want to drink.

Wandering entertainers with animals. The two rhesus monkeys are trained and dressed to perform a husband-and-wife act. The wanderoo (opposite page) is a pet taught to perform tricks.

Roadside entertainers with Himalayan black bear (left page), Brahmany kites (right) and leopard (below).

Crowd at religious ceremony gathers around cobra.

The spectacled cobra is the most feared of all snakes in India. Like all cobras, when it becomes excited it raises its body and forms a hood by pulling forward elongated ribs along the neck. This terrifying pose is accompanied by a hissing sound that is a prelude to the strike and venomous bite.

Cobras are found in the jungles and open fields and are not aggressive if some means of escape are open to them. But many of the people go about barefoot and the opportunities for being accidentally bitten are numerous. The cobra itself lives on mice, rats, frogs and toads, which it kills with its deadly bite.

The fight of the cobra and the mongoose is a classic drama often seen in India, and the outcome is largely the same. The mongoose is not immune to the venomous bite, but is faster and quicker in motion than the snake. The cobra assumes a posture of defense and attempts to reach the animal by a sweeping strike, but the quick-moving mongoose jumps out of reach and comes at the snake from another direction, before the snake can get into striking position again. This constant movement tires and discourages the snake, and the mongoose is finally able to leap in close and bury its teeth in the snake's neck, usually severing the joints of its vertebrae.

The chevrotain or mouse deer (below) is neither a mouse nor a deer but the smallest of the Asiatic hoofed animals. The size of a rabbit, it has fur like a fawn and a stubby tail, and lives all by itself in the forest; it never wanders from its protective cover, shyly coming out to feed at early dawn and dusk in order to avoid the many enemies that prey upon it.

The nilgai (left) is the largest of India's antelopes. The horned nilgai bulls are especially admired for their blue-grey color. The cows have no horns and are fawn-colored. These big antelopes are not shy; they invade the fields and damage the farmers' crops.

The dappled coat of the axis or chital deer of India makes them the most beautiful members of the deer family and provides them with camouflage protection. They move in herds of twenty to one hundred through the lowland forests, are very alert and at the least disturbance give warning to the others with a shrill cry.

Each spring in the rutting season the male black bucks test their strength. They hook their ringed and spiral horns and spar for hours. Black bucks are among the fastest runners in the animal world.

Female black bucks fleeing through the forest.

The wild gaur of India (left) lives in dense jungles in small herds made up of males or of cows and their young. In the mating season the bulls break up to gather a group of females which each bull protects from other males. The gaur is the tallest of the wild oxen, with horns sometimes up to 34 inches in length.

Above: A tame, young gaur.

The wild water buffalo is a dangerous though rare animal and is usually hunted from the back of an elephant for that reason. However, the majority of water buffalo have been domesticated for centuries and there is nothing more placid and docile. Small native children will boss the ton-heavy beasts around with a small switch. As their name implies, these animals are happiest when near water and if left to themselves would lie in water or mud wallows all day to escape the heat and the hordes of insects that plague them. Surprisingly enough, the young are not black like their parents but a dirty grey-white.

Here a native woman exhibits her water buffalo who possesses
a prize pair of horns—over 77 inches in length.

A domesticated water buffalo rests from his day's work.

Once a year, on the fifth day of the moon following the harvest of wheat, the people from the villages in Bharatpur gather at Sinsini for a three-day fair—a gay, colorful event in which dancing and singing alternate with wrestling competitions and racing of horses, camels and bullock carts.

Ylla visited the fair; the following pages give her impressions of it. The picture of the bullock-cart race which concludes the book is the last taken by Ylla. She was photographing the race from the hood of a slow-moving jeep when it struck an obstruction; Ylla fell from the jeep and was fatally injured.